The Pearson Connection

between
Leeds Metropolitan University
School of the Built Environment
and
S. Pearson & Son Ltd (Public Works Contractors)

Hugh Murray

Preface

By Jane Kettle
Head of School of the Built Environment
Leeds Metropolitan University

Anyone who ever attended a meeting held in the Pearson Room in Brunswick Terrace would have been surrounded by a colourful and imposing set of stained glass panels. But these works of art were usually behind closed doors, unacknowledged, anonymous and seldom regarded with anything but mild curiosity. At the end of 2005, the School of the Built Environment finally left Brunswick Terrace to take occupation of the imposing and elegant, new and refurbished accommodation in Queen Square Court. This building also provided a new home for the stained glass panels, which now form an impressive window installed along a corridor for all people using the building to see.

It wasn't until after the move that we in the School realised just what a rich piece of industrial and cultural heritage we have right in front of us. We were fortunate to be put in touch with Hugh Murray. Hugh, a chartered electrical engineer by profession, is a distinguished local historian with numerous publications on local historical material. Hugh's expertise in heraldry, and his previous acquaintance with the panels, made him the ideal person to approach to find out more about our windows, which we now know as the "Pearson Corridor". Hugh's lively and entertaining talk at the School's annual 'away day' traced both the historical and technological significance of the images shown in the glass, and the fascinating physical journey the windows have made between the early part of the 20th century to their relocation in 2005. The Pearson windows are a part of the University's rich heritage, and we are delighted that Hugh has been able to produce this excellent publication that explains and acknowledges their significance.

I would like to thank Hugh Murray, for his rigorous research and entertaining prose, Veronica Lovell and Barbara Mulroy for introducing us to Hugh, and to Rebecca Riley, Marie Haynes and, not least, Ian Dickinson, for their efforts in making this happen.

Contents

Introduction	1
S. Pearson & Son	2
The Whitehall Club	6
The Contracts (excluding Mexico)	14
The Contracts (Mexican)	24
Who's who in the windows	27
Heraldry and other devices	33
Pedigree of Pearson	37
Acknowledgements	38

Introduction

The Pearson Corridor

On 12 December 2005 the School of the Built Environment of Leeds Metropolitan University (formerly Leeds Polytechnic) moved into its new home in Queen Square Court, taking with it from its previous home 14 panels of stained glass now installed in one of the main circulating corridors of the building where they are lit by natural light from an internal courtyard.

In April 1979 these windows were installed in a pendecagonal room in the Brunswick Building. This building, owned by Leeds City Council, had been erected on the site of the former Gibraltar Barracks, a "splendid piece of Victorian military architecture". While the planning and erection of the new building was the responsibility of E.W. Stanley, the City Architect, the actual design was carried out by a member of his staff, David Wrightson, with the agreement of Dr Patrick Nuttgens, at that time Director of the Polytechnic. It was Wrightson's first design for a large scale building. He included this multi-faceted internal room, now known as the Pearson Room, in his design to accommodate the glass panels in 14 sides leaving the 15th for the door. The stained glass panels were a gift to the Polytechnic from Weetman John Churchill Pearson, 3rd Viscount Cowdray, the chairman of S. Pearson & Son Ltd. They were illuminated by indirect light from concealed fluorescent strip lights.

These panels use the medium of stained glass to portray the history of the firm of S. Pearson and Son Ltd from 1844 to, at least, 1927. While stained glass windows normally use imagery or symbolism, with a minimum of text, to portray their theme, these windows rely heavily on the written word to explain events and incorporations and to record engineering difficulties encountered in the contracts undertaken by the firm. They include portraiture, as well as civic and national heraldry and record the involvement of many of the great civil engineers of the day. The firm of S. Pearson & Son was clearly a major player in the field of Public Works in the late 19th and early 20th centuries but what are these windows recording its history doing in a building in Leeds?

Panels 6-9 and 10-13 in the Pearson Room

S. Pearson & Son

The founder of the firm was Samuel Pearson, a farmer from Scholes near Cleckheaton, who, in 1844, went into partnership with a builder from Huddersfield to undertake the building of reservoirs for Bowling Ironworks and the dyeworks of E. Ripley and Son, both firms located at Bowling, Bradford. In 1856 Samuel Pearson took his eldest son, George, into partnership as S. Pearson & Son. The new firm gained several local contracts at the waterworks at Dewsbury, Batley and Heckmondwike and a sewage works at Skipton and Tong. They were also concerned in the maintenance of the Lancashire and Yorkshire Railway, which had opened to Bradford in 1850, before assisting in new works to expand its system. During the construction of this railway a large quantity of surplus spoil was deposited on land adjoining Mill Lane, Bradford. As this material was suitable for brickmaking, the firm acquired it and established its Broomfield Brickworks there in 1860. The spoil heap, added to in 1865-6 when S Pearson & Son made a short branch for the GNR to enable that company to run its trains into Bradford Exchange Station, finally became exhausted after 25 years when the works were closed. The site was then used for housing. During its life the Broomfield Brickworks produced almost every variety of bricks, sanitary tubes and terra-cotta ware, importing finer clays as necessary.

With the opening of the brickyard the headquarters of the business was transferred to Bradford. As a consequence George Pearson moved his family there and briefly entered local politics as the councillor for Bowling in the Bradford Town Council from 1866 to 1869, later serving as a Poor Law Guardian in the Bradford Union. It is said "he took business lightly and pleasure seriously". Certainly his object seems to have been to raise his social standing. His gentrification was complete when in 1892 he received a Grant of Arms from the College of Arms. Samuel Pearson, still described as a brickmaker, retired in 1879 giving his share of the business to his grandson, Weetman Dickinson Pearson.

Weetman Dickinson Pearson had been educated at Pannal College, a boarding school near Harrogate but left in 1872 at the age of 16 to join the family firm. Here he learnt brickmaking and surveying and also took charge of contracts when his father was absent. Two years later, in 1874, he was put in charge of the Broomfield Brickworks and the following year was sent to the USA to seek new business. On his return home he was sent to Southport to superintend a £70,000 contract for a main drainage system. This was probably the most important contract so far undertaken by the firm and turned out, because of the waterlogged shifting subsoil, to be most difficult. It took three years to complete but young Weetman learned how to manage a work force in trying conditions and realised that contracts could be managed more effectively with a senior representative of the firm in residence on site. In 1879 he took charge of a £60,000 contract for a main drainage system at Ipswich and a £105,000 contract for a dock at Kings Lynn. It was here that his eldest son was born. When this latter contract was completed George Pearson became a director of the Kings Lynn Dock and Railway Board.

When Weetman Pearson became a director in 1879 he found that his father's easy going optimism had resulted in the firm extending its overdraft far beyond its means. The Ipswich and Kings Lynn contracts, however, under Weetman Pearson's careful management, restored the financial stability of the firm. In 1882 he secured a contract from the Metropolitan Board of Works for a storm water outfall at Deptford. Although only for £34,000 it enabled him to set about the expansion of the firm's activities on a national and international basis. Two years later he transferred the firm's headquarters from Bradford to London into an office in Delahay Street, Westminster and by 1888 to Victoria Street. George Pearson stayed behind at Bradford, and Weetman Pearson, in London, effectively took over the firm. On his father's retirement in 1895, two years after his move to a country estate at Brickendonbury, Hertfordshire, Weetman Pearson became the sole partner. His father died in 1899.

During the 1880s and 1890s S. Pearson & Son, still a private family firm, gained various contracts in the UK, Spain, Egypt, Brazil, Mexico, the USA and Canada for railways, drainage, docks and tunnels worth over £26 million . After Weetman Pearson was elected as an MP in 1895 the firm needed to be incorporated to allow it to apply for Government contracts. Accordingly in 1897 S. Pearson & Son Ltd was registered with a capital of £1,500,000. At first there was only one extra director, Clarendon Golding Hyde, a barrister who had worked for the firm since 1888, but by 1901 the board consisted of six, including three of his senior managers. By 1919 another four had joined the board, including two of his sons. This expansion in activity required additional offices in London and in 1906 the former premises of the Whitehall Club at 47 Parliament Street, Westminster, were acquired. Here the achievements of the firm, including an outline of its history, were displayed in panels of stained glass.

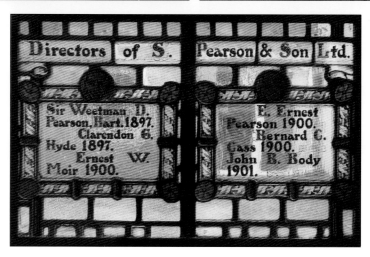

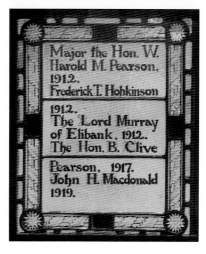

At the end of 1889 Weetman Pearson left New York, where he had been working on the Hudson River Tunnel, travelling on the Montezuma Express from New York to Mexico City at the invitation of the president of Mexico, General Porfirio Diaz, who wanted him to tender for the Grand Canal contract. In this he was successful and the £2 million contract awarded was the start of a very profitable association with that country. Contracts for port works and railways followed. In all they were worth over £10 million, 47% of the work the firm was engaged on in the 1890s. The association continued in the next decade with the establishment of electric power, light and tramway companies for five cities. But this was not the only benefit that Weetman Pearson gained from Mexico and the influence of its president. In 1901 he decided to enter the oil business and bought up land around Tehuantepec where oil seepage had been reported.

By 1906 he owned or had royalty leases on 900,000 acres of land. To exploit this asset the *Compania Mexicana de Petroleo El Aguila* (Mexican Eagle Oil Company) was formed in 1908, followed in 1912 in the UK by the Eagle Oil Transport Company and the Anglo-American Oil Company. This was an investment which paid handsomely starting with the Dos Bocas well in July 1908 which produced the largest oil gush on record. No wonder that General Porfirio Diaz is the only person, other than members of the Pearson family, whose portrait is displayed in the window. After the 1914-18 war Weetman Pearson withdrew from the oil business, which had not been as profitable as he had hoped, and sold his Mexican interests to the Royal Dutch Shell and the Shell Transport and Trading Companies.

Just as he was just about to embark on four railroad tunnels in New York, Weetman Pearson established S. Pearson & Son Inc. on 18 June 1904 to further his interests in the USA and enable him to undertake this contract. In the UK in 1907 he formed the Whitehall Securities Corporation to take over his non-contracting interests. This company used

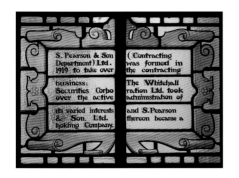

on its seal a representation of the Holbein Gate, which, between the 1530s and 1759, when it was demolished, had straddled Whitehall. The gate had also been used as the emblem of the Whitehall Club, whose building the firm now occupied. In 1919 S. Pearson & Son (Contracting Department) Ltd was formed to take over the contracting work and the original company, S. Pearson & Son Ltd, became a holding company which, two years later, acquired the group of companies which were to form the Westminster Press.

At the turn of the nineteenth century S. Pearson & Son was one of the leading, if not the leading, public works contractor in the country. Between 1900 and Weetman Pearson's death in 1927 the firm had contracts totalling over £25 millions, excluding the war work undertaken for the Government. His last great project was the Sennar Dam in the Sudan, built between 1923 and 1925 for £3,864,000. Weetman Pearson's success was due to many factors. Besides his personal qualities of fair-mindedness, generosity, integrity and willingness to heed advice, he ensured prosperity for his enterprises by hard work, persistence and personal involvement with all aspects of his undertaking. He took great pains to ensure the right costings, often making estimates independently of his staff. He thoroughly understood all the methods and machinery used. Each contract was treated as a separate entity so that the profit or loss of any aspect could be quickly and easily identified. He engendered loyalty among his managers by retaining them on a salary rather than dismissing them at the end of the contract as was the usual practice. His preference was for the 'measure and value' type of contract in which all items of work were detailed in the specification and a price was named for each of them. Little use was made of bank overdrafts, his work was largely self-financing as it was paid for on a regular monthly basis.

Despite this tremendous work load in managing the affairs of his own companies Weetman Pearson found time, somewhat reluctantly, to enter public life. After an unsuccessful attempt in 1892 he tried again and, with a baronetcy gained in 1894, was elected as Liberal MP for Colchester in 1895 and was made its High Steward in 1909. He was frequently absent from the House of Commons looking after his interests in Mexico which resulted in him being dubbed 'Member for Mexico'. He held Colchester until 1910 when was he was ennobled as Baron Cowdray of Midhurst, where he had two years earlier purchased Cowdray House and Park. In 1917, the year he became President of the Air Board, he was sworn as a Privy Councillor and promoted to a viscountcy as Viscount Cowdray of Cowdray. He gave Cowdray Park to his eldest son in 1919 and moved to Dunecht House in Aberdeenshire. He was elected Lord Rector of the University of Aberdeen the next year and was created a GCVO in 1925. When he died on 1 May 1927, full of honours, he was succeeded in the viscountcy by his eldest son, Weetman Harold Miller Pearson, and as chairman of S. Pearson & Son by his second son, Bernard Clive Pearson.

The armorial achievement of Viscount Cowdray. The personal arms of Pearson, granted to George Pearson in 1892, impale those of the viscountess, Annie, daughter of Sir John Cass. Lord Cowdray was granted the diver and Mexican peon as supporters when he became a baron in 1910.

Shortly before his death Viscount Cowdray decided that the contracting firm, S. Pearson & Son (Contracting Department) Ltd, should close on his demise as 'contracting was a one-man job'. The process of voluntary liquidation was completed in 1941 when £1 million was distributed amongst its shareholders. The parent company, S Pearson & Son Ltd, however, continued its role as a holding company. After the retirement of Bernard Clive Pearson in 1954 the chairmanship of the company passed to Weetman John Churchill Pearson, 3rd Viscount Cowdray. It was under his leadership, which lasted until 1977, that S. Pearson & Son Ltd expanded to become the media giant that it is today. First the *Financial Times* was purchased in 1957, followed by the Longman Press in 1968 and Penguin Books in 1970. Now under the name Pearson PLC it has expanded to include, amongst many other businesses, Addison Wesley, an American publisher, Dorling Kindersley and Rough Guides. Its portfolio, for a time, even included Madame Tussauds, Warwick Castle, Chessington Zoo and Alton Towers! All a far cry from the intentions of Samuel Pearson, the brickmaker of Scholes, who started it all.

The Whitehall Club - 47 Parliament Street (now 1 Derby Gate) Westminster

The first building erected on this site, latterly in the occupation of the Bahia Steam Navigation Company, was demolished in 1865, to be replaced by the present building. Although this was designed by Charles Octavius Parnell, (1807-1865), the architect of the Army and Navy Club, it was left, after his death, to his son, Charles Jocelyn Parnell to supervise its building by Messrs Lucas for a cost of £25,000. The Italianate building has Ionic pillars at ground floor level and Corinthian above surmounted by an elaborate cornice. It was built in 1866 for the Whitehall Club, an organisation chiefly composed of engineers, contractors and other gentlemen requiring to do business with Parliament or at the Government Offices nearby. It had a spacious morning room, 40 feet long, in the front of the ground floor with a coffee room of the same size behind. The accommodation on the first floor was a smoking room, a library and a billiard room. The kitchens were housed in the basements and the servants' quarters were in the attics.

In 1905 the Whitehall Club was in financial difficulties and, merging with another club in Storey's Gate, put up its building for sale. It was purchased in 1906 by Sir Weetman Dickinson Pearson, chairman of S. Pearson & Son, who was looking for extra space for his growing business. During the next two years the interior of the building was substantially altered, principally the staircase. The original masonry staircase was removed and replaced by stairs supported by exposed steel girders surrounding a central shaft for two electric lifts. The whole of the stairwell was clad in polished granite slabs. To proclaim his ownership Sir Weetman installed, in one of the first floor rooms, an over mantel bearing his heraldic achievement.

The entrance, in Derby Gate, to the Whitehall Club, surmounted by a sculpture designed by C.O. Parnell and sculpted by James Tolmie

This latter item, however, paled into insignificance compared with his other embellishment of the building. A window was installed on the south side of the staircase looking out in to a light well. This window was 9 feet wide and some 55 feet in height interrupted by girders at 40 degrees supporting the four flights of stairs. Sir Weetman, who was now claiming to be one of the country's leading contractors, used this window to demonstrate this fact to his clients. In stained glass panels, set in iron armatures, the history and engineering achievements of his firm were displayed for all who had the stamina to climb the staircase to see. Much of the glass dates from 1906/7 but two panels were installed, in or after 1912, to record later contracts. Sir Weetman's advance through the ranks of the peerage was noted in 1910 and 1917 and, after the First World War, panels were added to record the company's war work and Roll of Honour. Later contracts, including the building of the Sennar dam in the Sudan between 1923 and 1925, were not included, because of lack of space. A minor alteration was made in 1927 to record Lord Cowdray's death.

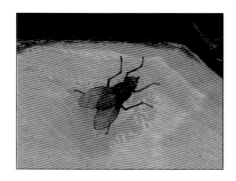

While two different styles can be detected in the glass painting the whole work was undertaken, at different periods, by Geoffrey Fuller Webb (1879-1954), the nephew of the architect, Sir Aston Webb. He trained at the Westminster School of Art and then joined Charles Eamer Kempe. He worked for a short time with Herbert Bryan before setting up his own studio in Brooker's Yard, East Grinstead. Some of his earliest work can be seen in the windows, depicting the history of the borough, in Woolwich Town Hall, built between 1903 and 1906. In his later years, certainly, he signed his work with a spider's web with the initials GW usually located in the bottom right hand corner of a window. There is no such signature in the surviving glass but the presence of a life-like fly in one of the lights may be a rebus, an arcane reference to the designer. Webb also painted some other windows for Weetman Dickinson Pearson. These were for the inner and outer halls of Paddockhurst (since 1933 Worth Abbey) at Worth near Crawley, the house which Pearson purchased in 1894. Sir Aston Webb was the architect for the additions and alterations to the house and must have introduced his nephew to his client.

Left:The top section of the window with portraits of the three generations of the Pearson family.
Right:The lower section of the window. The panel at the left has not survived.
Photographs courtesy of City of London, London Metropolitan Archives

The window at 47 Parliament Street was divided by the staircase risers into 5 areas. That at the top, with a maximum height of 10 feet, was genealogical and historical, portraying three generations of Pearson from Samuel, the founder, to Lord Cowdray himself and recording the history of the firm prior to and including its move into these offices. Most of the glass was painted in 1906 or the next year but some additions were subsequently made to include later events. The next flight down, of 10 ft average height and completed at one time, dealt with the firm's achievements in Mexico between 1889 and 1912. Below that a larger section of 15 feet average height recorded in the two side lights six significant contracts, started in or prior to 1906 while, originally, the centre light was left empty for future contracts. In the event it was used to record details of the firm's work in the first World War and its Roll of Honour of casualties. The only space remaining, at the bottom of the right hand light was used for two more contracts, both of 1912. Between the ground and first floor a 12ft high section gave details of more than 33 other contracts all dating from 1906 or before. Finally, at basement level, with a maximum height of six feet, were the insignia of the parent company and two associated companies, all founded by Lord Cowdray between 1897 and 1907, plus three more incorporations made in 1919.

1906 was a significant year for the firm. It had 13 contracts, amounting to nearly £10 million, in progress in Mexico, China, Columbia, USA and the British Isles. As a result no further work was taken on until 1909. This provided a clean cut-off point at which to end the record in stained glass of the firm's history and previous achievements. The very little space remaining was later all used up for the work in Mexico, two major contracts in 1912, the Royal Albert Dock Extension (£1,398,000) and Valparaiso Port Works in Chile (£2,710,000) and the firm's war work amounting to over £10 million. There was no room for the other 11 contracts started before the first World War and another 18 started between 1919 and 1926, including 3 worth over £1 million. It seems, therefore, that the window was intended only to commemorate events up to and including the acquisition of the Whitehall Club. While the small amount of spare space allowed the inclusion of a few extra significant contracts there can have been no plan to include the firm's work after 1906.

In the 1950s, with the Government desperate for more office space for MPs and civil servants, it was planned to pull down the whole eastern side of Parliament Street together with Cannon Row and Derby Gate and to replace them with new buildings. Negotiations, with the threat of compulsory purchase as the ultimate resort, were started with the owners in 1960 resulting in the purchase of 47 Parliament Street by the Ministry of Works in May 1963. The question of the retention of the stained glass window had been raised at a meeting in January 1962 when it was agreed that it should remain the property of S. Pearson & Son. No immediate move was made to remove the window and it remained *in situ* gracing the Welsh Office, the new occupant of the building from 1966. Then in 1971, a year before the Welsh Office moved out to be replaced by the Supplementary Benefits Tribunal, the current Viscount Cowdray decided to reclaim his property.

He wanted to find a new home for not only the window but also his firm's contract archives. He contacted the Business Archives Council (BAC), then under the presidency of Lord Denning, Master of the Rolls, for advice. Knowing the Yorkshire origins of S. Pearson & Son, the secretary of the BAC, Major T.L. Ingram, sought the help of Dr Joyce Bellamy of the Department of Economics and Commerce in the University of Hull. She had, the previous year, published *Yorkshire Business Histories - A Bibliography* and was an eminently suitable person to consult. Her advice was to offer the window and the archive to Leeds Polytechnic. Accordingly Ingram wrote to Dr Patrick Nuttgens on 26 January 1971 suggesting this, and, importantly, informing him that S. Pearson & Son Ltd would meet the cost of removing and restoring the window and installing it in its new home where it should be made available for public viewing.

The staircase between the first and second floors of 47 Parliament Street in 1973 after the painted glass had been removed

Dr Bellamy could not have suggested a better person to approach. Not only was Dr Nuttgens enthusiastic about the possibility of having the window but his father, Joseph Edward Nuttgens (1892-1982) and his brother, Joseph Ambrose Nuttgens (1941-) were stained glass artists. After visiting 47 Parliament Street with his father, Dr Nuttgens reported that the window was well worth preserving although the bottom section was in very bad condition with several sections broken. Otherwise the only other problem was some buckling due to the age of the lead cames. There were two possibilities for relocating it in Leeds. The Polytechnic was in process of acquiring a Victorian building but plans were in the early stages for a totally new building to house Architecture, Building, Civil Engineering and Town Planning. It would be a fairly simple task to incorporate the fully restored panels into this building which was expected to be ready in 1974.

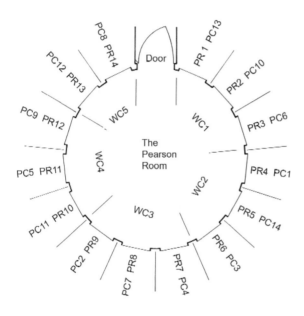

The Pearson Room showing the previous location of the panels in the Whitehall Club and, subsequently, in the Pearson Corridor.
Key: WC - Whitehall Club PR - Pearson Room PC - Pearson Corridor

This positive report resulted in S. Pearson & Son making a formal offer in May 1971 to give the window to Leeds Polytechnic for the proposed new building. The firm also commissioned Goddard & Gibbs Studios of Shoreditch, Stained Glass Makers, Restorers and Conservators, to remove the window from 47 Parliament Street and prepare it for its new home. Although the ex-Whitehall Club was given Grade II* listed status on 18 February 1972, Lord Cowdray enforced his previously agreed right of removal which was completed by the end of March 1973. This listed status caused Parliament to review its plans for the development of the site. A feasibility study, presented in November 1983, concluded that the existing buildings on the site could be retained within a scheme which would provide all the required new accommodation. Thus, since 1991, 47 Parliament Street, now renamed 1 Derby Gate, houses part of the House of Commons Library but MPs and others using its facilities can only look at the window apertures on the stairwell filled with plain plate glass.

Having had the gift of the windows to Leeds Polytechnic confirmed the decisions about its new home could be made. E.W. Stanley, the City Architect, thought the window should not be incorporated into a public area as that might lend undue importance to S. Pearson & Son Ltd suggesting a closer connection with the Polytechnic than actually existed. Rather it should located in a seminar or meeting room where it could be back-lit to provide background lighting similar to that provided by an existing mural in a meeting room in the Spanish department. There was 408 square feet of glass to accommodate and by rearranging it into 10

9

panels, each four feet wide, only a small amount of plain glazing would be lost allowing a 40 feet display on one wall of a large room. Dr Nuttgens favoured covering two or three walls of a smaller room. The solution eventually reached was the 15-sided Pearson Room, with no external windows. The remaining problem was how to arrange glass from parallelogram shaped windows in a way that preserved its original logic. The solution was to create 14 rectangular panels 3 feet wide and 8 feet in height, each headed by a round topped panel, and allocate each group of three consecutive lights to each level of the parent window starting at the left of the door and continuing round in a clockwise direction. This required a certain amount of rearrangement, and in the case of the three middle levels the loss of some glass. That there were originally 15 round-topped panels means that one from the bottom level has been lost, presumably part of one of the broken sections noticed by Dr Nuttgens. In all 72 square feet (18%) of glass has not survived the rearrangement, particularly pictorial glass from the Mexican section, 12 panels representing some of the smaller contracts, the record of the company's war work and its Roll of Honour. It is not known what has happened to this discarded glass.

The fifteenth, and now missing, round top window in 1971. It commemorates the incorporation of S. Pearson & Son Ltd in 1897.

The Pearson stained glass was formally welcomed into its new home on 29 April 1979 by Viscount Cowdray on the occasion of the opening of the Brunswick Building by Sir Hugh Casson whose firm, Casson Conder, had been consulting architects for the Parliament Street Buildings in London. The archives of S. Pearson & Son, had not been wanted by Leeds Polytechnic and found their new home, perhaps more appropriately, in the Science Museum in South Kensington. Twenty-six years later the glass was moved to its third home in Queen Square Court.

The Staff Magazine of the House of Commons Library - Vol 6 No 6, Christmas 2000 - has an article about the Pearson Stained Glass Window which concludes: "If Leeds Metropolitan University ever demolish the Brunswick Building, wouldn't it be nice to bring the glass home, to commemorate the connection between our building and one of the foremost contracting firms of the last 150 years?"

Disregarding the fact that some 18% of the stained glass has disappeared in the move north, this is wishful thinking. While the Brunswick Building is to be demolished, the windows have found a new and, it is to be hoped, permanent home in Leeds, still in the care of the School of the Built Environment, which has been the custodian of the stained glass since 1979.

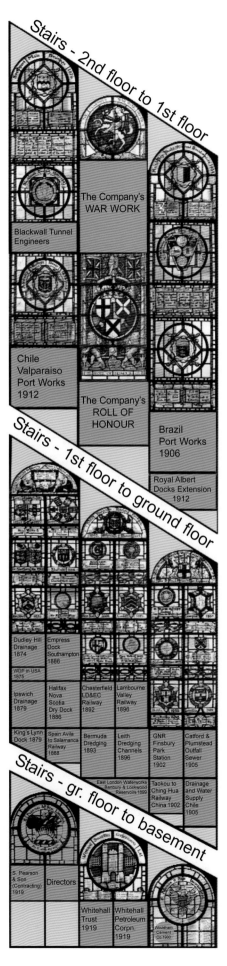

Stairs - 2nd floor to 1st floor

Stairs - 3rd floor to 2nd floor

Stairs - 2nd floor to 1st floor

Stairs - 1st floor to ground floor

Stairs - gr. floor to basement

Oil Gusher

Vera Cruz & Mazatlan Water Supply and Drainage

Power Stations

Refineries

Oil Tanker

The Company's WAR WORK

Blackwall Tunnel Engineers

Chile Valparaiso Port Works 1912

The Company's ROLL OF HONOUR

Brazil Port Works 1906

Royal Albert Docks Extension 1912

Dudley Hill Drainage 1874

Empress Dock Southampton 1886

WDP in USA 1875

Ipswich Drainage 1879

Halifax Nova Scotia Dry Dock 1886

Chesterfield LD&EC Railway 1892

Lambourne Valley Railway 1896

King's Lynn Dock 1879

Spain Avila to Salamanca Railway 1888

Bermuda Dredging 1893

Leith Dredging Channels 1896

GNR Finsbury Park Station 1902

Catford & Plumstead Outfall Sewer 1905

East London Waterworks Banbury & Lockwood Reservoirs 1899

Taokou to Ching Hua Railway China 1902

Drainage and Water Supply Chile 1905

S. Pearson & Son (Contracting) 1919

Directors

Whitehall Trust 1919

Whitehall Petroleum Corpn. 1919

Wouldham Cement Co.1900

A reconstruction of the window at 47 Parliament Street as it was in 1971. The panels highlighted in blue did not survive the move from London to Leeds.

The panels rearranged for display in the Pearson Room in 1979. Each group of three lights corresponds with a level at 47 Parliament Street except for the lowest level where only two lights survive. Some 18% of the glass has been lost in making the panels fit the space available.

The panels rearranged, in four groups of 3,4,4,3, after installation in their present home in 2005. There is no longer any logic in the order in which they are displayed.

The Contracts (excluding Mexico)

1844-1854 Reservoirs for Bowling Iron Co & Ripley & Son, [Dyers]

Both these companies used, for their processes, large quantities of water which Bradford Corporation found difficult to supply. The solution was the construction of reservoirs on their premises. After the work was complete Ripley & Son could store 1,250,000 gallons of water.

1854-1877 Dewsbury Waterworks and sundry water and gas contracts

Contracts included waterworks for Dewsbury, Batley and Heckmondwike, sewage works at Uppingham, Skipton and Tong, a main sewer extension at Doncaster and reservoirs at Staincliffe and Horton Park.

Lancashire And Yorks Railway, New Works and General Maintenance 1857- 1877

This contract was a considerable prize for the firm involving both the construction of new lines for the railways rapidly expanding system across the Pennines and for the upkeep of a section of line in Yorkshire.

The railway company, in common with many others in these early days of railway expansion, chose to show its territorial aspirations in designing its heraldic device. Unfortunately, at this time neither Lancashire nor Yorkshire had armorial bearings so the arms of the two county towns were used, although the company's lines never reached Lancaster

Great Northern Railway 1865

The window at 47 Parliament Street originally had 2 panels referring to work for the GNR. The 1865 panel has been lost and replaced by the 1902 panel. The work referred to, for which James Fraser was the engineer, was commissioned by the Leeds, Bradford and Halifax Railway, which soon afterwards was absorbed into the GNR, to enable the company's trains to run into Bradford Exchange Station rather than Adolphus Street Station, which was too far out of town.

The armorial device of the GNR also expresses territorial ambitions although to go further north than Doncaster it had to negotiate running powers over the lines of other companies.

Bradford Waterworks, Oxenhope Tunnel, 1870 - £15,000

In 1842 Bradford Waterworks was formed, by Act of Parliament, to supply the town with water. Its supplies, from Manywells in the Hewenden valley, proved to be insufficient so in 1854 Bradford Corporation obtained an Act authorising it to purchase the Waterworks for £215,000 and take over the powers the company had obtained to draw water from the watersheds of the rivers Aire and Wharfe. After completing this scheme the Corporation extended its operations into the watersheds of the Hewenden valley. As a part of this latter work a massive stone conduit was constructed under Thornton Moor into the Worth Valley near Oxenhope.

Dudley Hill, Bradford, Drainage 1874
Panel lost in the transfer of the glass from London to Leeds

Southport Main Drainage 1876 - £70.000

Weetman Dickinson Pearson, grandson of the founder of S. Pearson & Son, was put in charge of this difficult contract at the age of 20 as the firm's representative on site. Southport is built on sand and, with a waterlogged, shifting sub-soil, it was difficult to provide a durable bed for the sewers. The work took three years to complete and taught him more about contracting work than almost any subsequent contract. He had had to take charge of a considerable body of workmen which he handled with 'tact and discretion'.

Ipswich Main Drainage 1879 - £360,000
King's Lynn Dock 1879 - £105,000
Panels lost in the transfer of the glass from London to Leeds

Deptford Storm Water Sewer 1882- £34,000

Sir Joseph Bazalgette's interception sewer scheme for London (1859-1874), although removing the raw sewage from the Thames which caused 'the Great Stink', had not made provision for abnormal quantities of storm water caused by heavy rainfall. When the sewage and rainfall reached a certain height in the new sewers it overflowed into the old ones and was discharged directly into the Thames within the metropolis. After 1879 several relief sewers were constructed by the Metropolitan Board of Works to carry this excess storm water. The Deptford sewer was five eighths of a mile in length.

The arms surrounding the Royal achievement are, clockwise, starting at one o'clock, those of Guildford (representing Surrey), Westminster, Colchester (representing Essex), Kent, London and Middlesex - derived from the Seal of the Metropolitan Board of Works.

Sheffield Main Drainage 1884 - £144,700

A scheme for Sheffield Corporation which took until 1887 to complete.

Milford Haven Docks 1885 - £120,000

Milford Haven was 200 miles nearer the USA than any other British port, and, with its deep water and sheltered harbourage, was very suitable for the Atlantic trade. S. Pearson & Son constructed for the Milford Dock Company a graving [dry] dock 700 feet long and wet docks capable of accommodating 12 big transatlantic liners at any one time. Despite these facilities Milford Haven was never able to wrest the superiority from Southampton, which the next year commissioned the firm to construct an 8 acre deep water dock.

Halifax, Nova Scotia, Graving Dock 1886 - £270,000
Southampton, Empress Dock 1886 - £210,000
Panels lost in the transfer of the glass from London to Leeds

Portsea Torpedo Range 1887 - £30,000
Devonport Slipway 1898 - £13,000

Portsea Torpedo Range marked the beginning of an association between S. Pearson & Son and the Admiralty. A dockyard of 8 acres was established here c1540 and by 1865 it had grown to 293 acres. Subsequent improvements in the 19th century included a torpedo range in the harbour as well as 2 new dry docks (1896) and a coal wharf with hydraulic loading equipment.

The Devonport slipway has been included on this panel, although out of chronological order, to save space.

Spain, Avila to Salamanca Railway 1888 - £950,000
Panel lost in the transfer of the glass from London to Leeds

Alexandria, dredging for entrance channel 1889 - £83,000

To improve the entrance to Alexandria Harbour a straight channel was cut through solid rock 300 feet wide to a depth of 30 feet. A rock-dredger, capable of lifting 400 tons of rock per hour, was specially designed by Simons & Co. of Renfrew. Over a three year period it removed 30,000 cubic feet of rock ensuring the channel was cut to specification.

Hudson River Tunnel, New York 1889 - £235,000

An earlier attempt to tunnel under the mile wide, fast flowing Hudson River was abandoned in 1887 after reaching 2,000 feet when silt inundated the advanced workings killing over 20 men. In 1889 S. Pearson & Son were invited to complete the work. The method it chose was a combination of a tunnelling shield driven through the silt and compressed air to prevent the silt squeezing through into the forward workings. The air pressure of between 35 to 37 pounds per square inch was maintained by a power plant on the river bank and piped to an air lock 100ft from the face through which the pressure could be controlled to prevent the workmen emerging suffering from the bends. After 18 months, when a further 2,000 feet had been completed, funds ran out and the workings were sealed. Ten years later the tunnel was completed by another firm.

GWR South Devon Widening 1890 - £83,000
GWR South Wales Direct Line 1897 - £1,300.000

Twelve miles of line between Brent, Hemerdon, Ivybridge and Cornwood were doubled and changed from broad gauge to standard gauge. Five viaducts, with 50 arches at an average height of 90 feet, the highest 120 feet, had to be strengthened and widened. Over 4,000,000 bricks were required.

The 1897 contract was for the construction of a new line from Wootton Bassett to Patchway. Avoiding the curve through Bath and Bristol it shortened the journey from London to South Wales by 11 miles. It was 33 miles in length with four viaducts, 100 bridges and three tunnels. Because of unforeseen difficulties, especially in one of the tunnels, the contract overran by £457,000. After a case for compensation reached the House of Lords judgement was given against the firm. Pearson thought he had been treated with scant consideration and never again tendered for any work for the GWR.

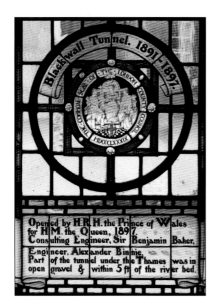

Blackwall Tunnel 1891-1897 - £871,000

With no river crossing, other than ferries, available downstream of Tower Bridge an Act of Parliament was obtained in 1887 to construct a tunnel at Blackwall. Sir Joseph Bazalgette prepared a scheme for the Metropolitan Board of Works for three parallel bores. The Board was replaced in March 1890 by the LCC and its engineer, Alexander Binnie, produced a design for a single bore tunnel, the sub aqueous part 3,694 feet long and 24 feet 3 inches in diameter. It was constructed using the shield and compressed air system perfected on the Hudson River tunnel. As well as London clay it passed through a section of water bearing ballast and gravel, in one stretch no more than five feet below the river bed. This problem could not be avoided by lowering the tunnel as its position was dictated by the gradient of the approaches which had to be negotiated by the horse drawn vehicles of the time. The tunnel was opened on 22 May 1897.

Lancashire, Derby & East Coast Railway 1892 - £1,035,00
Bermuda, Rock Dredging 1893 - £50,000
Panels lost in the transfer of the glass from London to Leeds

Surrey Commercial Docks, Dock Extensions
1895 - £164,000, 1898 - £470,000

The Surrey Docks in Rotherhithe were originally occupied by many different companies, trading in commodities such as timber, hemp, flax, tar, grain, salt, fruit, cheese, bacon and coal. After the formation of the Surrey Commercial Dock Company in 1807, timber and grain became the staple produce traded there. Greenland Dock was bought in 1808, refurbished and renamed Commercial Dock. Construction work to widen it began in 1895 and was completed in 1908. At its peak the system comprised 10 docks covering 372 acres.

Cardiff Dry Docks 1895 - £1,000,000

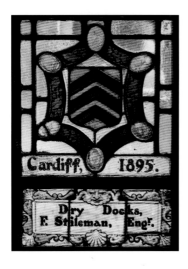

These dry docks were built for Cardiff Channel Dry Dock and Pontoon Company, one of several organisations established to provide ship-repairing facilities at Cardiff and Barry Docks.

The coat of arms used to represent this contract was an unofficial one. Cardiff did not get a formal grant of arms until 1906.

Port Talbot Railway & Dock 1895 - £720,000

Christopher Rice Mansel Talbot (1803-1890) was a wealthy landowner who established an ironworks on his property at Aberafan in 1831. His daughter, Emily Charlotte Talbot (1840-1918), inherited her father's fortune and used it to develop a port, to become known as Port Talbot, and a railway system to attract business away from Cardiff and Swansea. The work for the Port Talbot Railway and Dock Company was completed in 1900.

The heraldic symbol used to represent the contract is the crest of the Talbot family together with a motto describing the company's sphere of activities. Port Talbot did not get its own coat of arms until 1953.

Lambourne Valley Light Railway 1896 - £125,000
Leith Harbour Dredging 1896 - £40,000
Panels lost in the transfer of the glass from London to Leeds

GN & City Railway, Electric Underground Railway, Moorgate Station, City 1898 - £2,457,000

The object of this railway was to remove the difficulties travellers experienced in getting from the north of London to the City by constructing a three and a half mile tunnel from Finsbury Park to Finsbury Pavement. Not only did S. Pearson & Son undertake the work of contractor but also acted as promoter, floating a company with a capital of £2,000,000. When the work was completed in 1906 it ran the line for three years before selling it to the Metropolitan Railway Company.

Admiralty Harbour Dover 1898 - £3,365,000

Since the invention of the torpedo the Downs were no longer a safe anchorage for the fleet and a properly constructed harbour at Dover became a necessity. It involved the building of three breakwaters 9,520 feet in total length, 40 feet in width and the average depth of foundations 47 feet below low water at spring tides rising another 33 feet to the promenade level. Some 52,000 concrete blocks with granite facings and weighing 20 to 40 tons each were cast during the construction of the breakwaters. To ensure continuity of supplies Wouldham Cement Works and Gunnislake Granite Quarry were purchased. In all 610 acres were enclosed, 322 having a depth of at least 30 feet. With these dimensions it was the largest artificial harbour in the world. It took 11 years to complete.

East London Waterworks, Banbury & Lockwood Reservoirs 1899 - £338,000
Panel lost in the transfer of the glass from London to Leeds

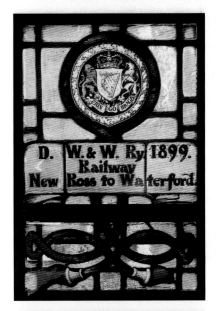

New Ross & Waterford Railway, New Ross to Waterford 1899 - £150,000

The Waterford, Wexford, Wicklow and Dublin Railway Company was incorporated by Act of Parliament in 1846. It changed its name to the Dublin, Wicklow and Wexford Railway Company in 1860. The extension from New Ross to Waterford was made to provide a connection with the Great Southern & Western Railway which, in turn, gave it access to the south of Ireland.

Seaham Harbour 1899 - £378,000

The Marquess of Londonderry acquired the Seaham estate in 1821 and began to extend the mining of coal there. To facilitate the export of coal, a harbour was built in 1831 and expanded in 1835 and 1845. In 1898 the Londonderry port and coal interests were separated with the formation of the Seaham Harbour Dock Company whose object was to raise funds for a major extension to the south dock. This new body engaged S. Pearson & Son Ltd to enlarge the harbour by building two masonry piers 1383 and 878 feet long together with an eight acre dock. This was one of the few lump sum contracts undertaken by the firm who finished up £50,000 in the red having failed to take account of the violence of the North Sea.

The device representing this contract is heraldic in origin, *four ermine spots conjoined in cross*, but has not been identified. Possibly it is part of the seal of the dock company or the insignia of the marquess. Seaham itself did not get a grant of arms until 1951.

Dublin Main Drainage Outfall 1900 - £120,000

At the end of the 19th century funds for the improvement of public facilities in Dublin were wholly provided by the municipality. To improve the primitive system of sanitation that existed, money had to be diverted from the re-planning of the city's streets to provide proper drainage and other services. The new main drainage system was opened in 1906 and rapidly extended to districts outside the municipal boundary.

Malta, Dry Docks 1903 - £625,000, Breakwaters 1904 - £500,000

Two new dry docks were constructed at the head of the French Creek in Valetta Harbour, one a double dock 790 feet long, with a caisson in the centre, and the other a single dock 550 feet long. During the excavations for the docks several fissures were struck through which sea water poured at an average rate of 32 million gallons a day, sometimes reaching 45 million gallons, for a period of 5 months. Powerful and very expensive pumps had to be installed setting the completion of the work back by two years. As a result the firm was out of pocket by £265,000 which the Admiralty refused, despite arbitration, to reimburse claiming it was 'contractors' risk'.

The breakwaters were twice damaged during their construction by hurricane force storms making much rebuilding necessary.

GNR, Finsbury Park Underground Station 1902 - £101,000
China, Taokou to Ching Hua Railway 1902 - £500,000
Panels lost in the transfer of the glass from London to Leeds

Liverpool, Queens Branch Dock 1902 - £340,000

Queens Dock was built in 1785 and was extended in 1902 by a branch dock 880 feet by 247 feet, and a graving dock 630 feet by 80 feet. In addition a river wall 770 feet long was built in front of them. Since 1972, having been filled in with hardcore and hard surfaced, these docks have become a car park.

The device used to represent this contract is taken from the seal of Liverpool Docks. From 1708 until 1811 the Docks had used the Corporation seal but they were, in this latter year, separately incorporated with their own seal.

Plymouth, Main Sewer Outfall 1903 - £28,000

A contract undertaken for Plymouth Corporation which was completed in 1906.

Pennsylvania Railroad, New York, Tunnel 1904 - £3,500,000

The scheme required the construction of four tunnels, each 23 feet in diameter, to cross the East River in an almost straight line and continuing 2,000 feet under Long Island, a total of 24,704 feet. The conditions differed materially from the soft silt of the Hudson River and the gravel of the Thames. The bed of the East River consisted of rock of a treacherous and varying quality, a compound of rock and quicksand and decomposed schist. The system of compressed air and shield was used with the difference that the rock in front of the shield had to be blasted out before the shield could be advanced and the cast iron liners installed behind. The work was completed in 1909.

The emblems representing this contract are:
Top   The arms of New York City
Left   The seal of the Pennsylvania Railroad Co
Right   The seal of S. Pearson & Son Inc.
Bottom   The seal of the Pennsylvania, New York & Long Island Railroad Co

Columbia, Dorada Railway Extension 1905 - £250,000

The Dorada Extension Limited was incorporated in 1905 with an authorised capital of £350,000, being a reconstitution of the Dorada Limited which owned a concession from the Chilean Government for a railway 23 miles long. Later the same year the new company acquired an additional concession for an extension to Girardot. In all 71 miles of 3 foot gauge railway was built.

LCC Catford to Plumstead Main Outfall Sewer 1905 - £450,000
Chile, Punta Arenas Drainage and Water Supply 1905 - £65,000
Panels lost in the transfer of the glass from London to Leeds

Hull Joint Dock 1906 - £1,334,000

In 1906 the Hull Joint Dock Committee, formed by the NER and the Hull & Barnsley Railway, obtained an Act of Parliament to construct a new dock to handle the coal exports of the two companies. The main basin was 1,000 feet by 1,050 feet with two large arms on the north-west and north-east, 1,350 feet by 325 feet and 1,365 feet by 450 feet respectively. An entrance lock 750 feet by 85 feet was also built. The completed dock was opened on 26 June 1914 by King George V whereupon it was renamed the King George Dock. It was the best equipped coal dock in the country.

The armorial device was specially devised, presumably because a combination of the heraldry of the parent companies would have been excessively complicated. It consisted of the arms of Hull in base and, in chief, a locomotive with the letters NE&HBR on its tender.

Brazil, Para Port Works 1906 - £2,100,000
Chile, Valparaiso Port Works 1912 - £2,710,000
PLA, Royal Albert Dock Extension 1912 - £1,398,000
Panels lost in the transfer of the glass from London to Leeds

The Company's War Works 1914-1918

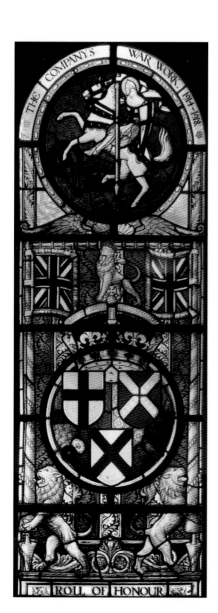

The descriptive panel detailing the works carried out for the Government, as well as the list of company's employees who fell in the war, has been lost in the rearrangement of the glass to fit its new home in Leeds.

The largest project, running from 1915 to 1918, was the general superintendence of the building of a munitions factory at Gretna together with an industrial town capable of housing 15,000 to 20,000 workers and providing them with all the necessities of life. A large part of the construction of the plant, which included 78 miles of standard gauge and 47 miles of two foot gauge railway as well as a power house with 10.5 megawatt capacity, was carried out by S. Pearson & Son Ltd who received £9,184,000 for both its construction work and the supervision of all the other works.

Also in 1915 anti-submarine defences were built at Dover and at Wallett in the mouth of the Thames while, in the Humber, forts were built at Sunk Island and Stallingborough.

Finally in 1918 a start was made on the construction of a tank assembling factory at Chateauroux in France capable of turning out 1,500 tanks per month. The war ended before the factory was finished.

The Contracts (Mexican)

Grand Canal 1889 - £2,000,000

The Valley of Mexico, an immense basin of 2,220 square miles, over 7,000 feet above sea level and surrounded by rocky mountains, had no rivers leading out of it. Rainwater ran into a chain of lakes which relied on seepage and evaporation to maintain their levels. However during the wet season every year more water accumulated which, for a time, inundated settlements. The earliest solution to this problem was a tunnel 10 miles long constructed in 1607. This soon collapsed but an earthquake in 1634 produced a fissure through which the excess water temporarily drained. The next solution, completed in the 17th century, was a cutting through the mountains 14 miles long, 400 feet wide and 180 feet deep. Although this prevented much flooding, Mexico City was still occasionally inundated because the bottom of the cutting was 30 feet above the level of the lowest lake. In the middle of the 19th century it was proposed to build a new tunnel leading to the Gulf of Mexico together with a drainage canal. After four years of work on the canal, which started in 1885, the contract to make it was rescinded and S. Pearson & Son was invited to tender and was awarded a new contract.

Work started in January 1890 using five dredgers designed by Frederick Lobnitz of Renfrew, Weetman Dickinson Pearson's brother-in-law. The largest could dredge to a depth of 50 feet, the string of buckets was 150 feet in length and the chutes at either side were capable of projecting the waste material 200 feet from the dredger. In all, by the time the work was completed in June 1896, 15,000,000 cubic yards of spoil had been excavated from a canal over 29 miles in length. The firm was paid sometimes in Mexican Internal Bonds, sometimes in Treasury notes and sometimes in silver bullion from Mexican mines. The goodwill engendered by the successful completion of this contract ensured much future work in Mexico for the firm.

Vera Cruz Harbour 1895 - £3,000,000

When the firm was importing its materials for the Grand Canal it had great difficulties in landing them at Vera Cruz, an open roadstead exposed to the full force of the north winds. Work on a small breakwater had been started but was abandoned because it had affected the currents causing the harbour to silt up. A bolder and more comprehensive scheme was formulated requiring the harbour be deepened to 8.5 metres, in some places to 10 metres, the existing breakwater to be completed and two more to be built. A space of 450 acres was thus enclosed in which an 800 metre long masonry jetty and two 180 metre long iron jetties were constructed for ocean traffic. The north-west seawall was to be completed in two and a half years, accommodation provided for discharging six large liners in four years and the whole completed in five years. A total of 247 acres was claimed from the sea during the course of the work which was subsequently used for sidings, warehouses, and public buildings.

The Mexican Government

In 1550 the Portuguese navigator, Antonio Gavao, published a book to show that a canal could be built at Tehuantepec, Nicaragua or Panama to link the Atlantic and Pacific ocean. It was not, however, until 1771 that the Spanish Government ordered a survey at Tehuantepec which showed that a canal was impractical as it involved climbing the 700 feet high Sierra Madre ridge. This was no obstacle to a railway which, after many false starts, was completed in 1897 but was so flimsily built that it could not possibly carry the heavy traffic that would be generated by an ocean to ocean link. President Diaz invited Weetman Dickinson Pearson to advise him on what was required. Pearson, on making a survey in 1899, saw that improving the railway was not sufficient. Deep-water ports were required at each end of the line. Accordingly he proposed to the Mexican Government a new type of contract under which he would reconstruct the railway and construct the ports. He also undertook to establish maritime services, and, under a 50 year contract, to run the railway and harbours. This was readily agreed and the deed of partnership was signed on 18 November 1899.

Isthmus of Tehuantepec - Harbours 1899-1909, Salina Cruz - £3,3000,000, Puerto Mexico - £1,400,000

Salina Cruz, on the Pacific coast, was situated in a wide open bay with only a little shelter from cliffs on the eastern side. Breakwaters were constructed to enclose an outer space and a dock wall running across this space created an inner sheltered harbour. The facilities provided included wharves and warehouses and a dry dock 666 feet long and 72 feet wide. To complete the work a new town, with proper drainage and water supply, was laid out on the hillside above the port.

At Coatzacoalas, renamed Puerto Mexico, on the Atlantic side, the problem was easier. It lay on a broad navigable river with deep water except at the entrance where there was a bar with only 14 feet clearance at high tide. A channel 328 feet wide and 33 feet deep was dredged through the bar, lined by two new rock jetties which confined the tides, ensuring that natural scouring would prevent the bar reforming. Inside was a deep basin where a mile and a quarter of deep water wharves were constructed along the river bank. The new town at the port was supplied with good drainage and pure water.

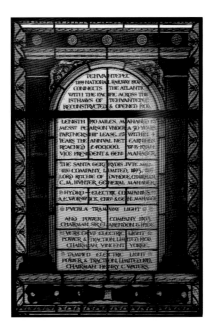

Tehuantepec National Railway 1898 - £2,500,000

To provide the link between the two new ports and carry the heavy cargoes required something better than the railway opened in 1897. Surveys, however, revealed that it followed the best route. The peninsula was 140 miles wide but the railway line required to make the crossing was 190 miles long rising to 852 feet above sea level at its highest point. With the route determined S. Pearson & Son Ltd reduced gradients, straightened curves, replaced wooden viaducts with steel ones and re-laid the track with heavier rails on proper ballast. All this had to be done with as little as possible interruption to the daily services of the existing railway.

The railway and ports were inaugurated with a ceremony on 25 January 1907 presided over by President Diaz. The commercial results of the line far exceeded expectations and the line maintained its services up to the first years of the first World War. In 1918 the Mexican Government decided, within the terms of its agreement, to wind up the partnership, and take on, on its own, the competition from the Panama Canal which had opened on 15 August 1914. Under Mexican management, however, both the railway and the harbours fell into disrepair and, being unable to develop any new business, could not compete with a system that did not require any transhipment of cargoes.

Santa Gertrudis Jute Mill Company Ltd 1893

This was an enterprise at Orizaba in which Weetman Dickinson Pearson was associated with his brother-in-law, Thomas Francis Kinnell, husband of Gertrude Cass, who, in 1892, made a $2,000,000 investment in jute. In the early years of the 20th century electric power plant was installed which trebled the capacity of the mill.

Hydro-Electric Companies
Peulba Tramway Light & Power Company 1903
Vera Cruz Electric Light Power & Traction Ltd 1906
Tampico Electric Light Power & Traction Ltd 1912

In 1902 Weetman Dickinson Pearson recruited A.E. Worswick, a Canadian electrical engineer who had just completed an electric tramway system for Mexico City, to launch a series of hydro-electric power companies.

Vera Cruz Drainage and Water Supply 1901 - £400,000
Panel lost in the transfer of the glass from London to Leeds

Mazatlan Drainage 1906 - £60,000
Panel lost in the transfer of the glass from London to Leeds

Who's who in the windows

(Information in italics appears in the windows)

Adam, Robert

i/c Mexican Government Isthmus of Tehuantepec Harbours at Salina Cruz and Puerto Mexico (Coatzacoalcos) 1899-1909.

Adams, Fred

i/c Mexican Government Isthmus of Tehuantepec Harbours at Salina Cruz and Puerto Mexico, (Coatzacoalcos) 1899-1909.

Baker, Benjamin, Sir

Engineer River Hudson Subaqueous tunnels New York 1889.
Consulting Engineer Blackwall Tunnel 1891-1897.
KCMG 1890 KCB 1902. Joint Engineer of Forth Railway Bridge.
Son of Benjamin Baker of Carlow, born 1840 and died 19 May 1907.

Barry, J. Wolfe, Sir

Engineer Surrey Commercial Dock Extensions 1895 & 1898.
KCB 1897, President ICE 1896-7. Engineer of Tower Bridge, completed 1894, Engineer of Caledonian, Barry, London Chatham & Dover, Metropolitan and District Railways.
Son of Sir Charles Barry RA, born 1836 and died 22 Jan 1918.

Bazalgette, Joseph William, Sir

Engineer Deptford Storm Water Sewer 1882.
Kt Bach 1874, President ICE 1888, Chief Engineer of Metropolitan Board of Works 1856-1889. Designer of Thames Embankment and associated sewage works as well as several parks, streets and three bridges in London.
Son of Joseph William Bazalgette RN, born 28 March 1819 and died 15 March 1891.

Binnie, Alexander Richardson

Engineer, Blackwall Tunnel 1891-1897.
K Bach 1897 President ICE 1905, Engineer City of Bradford 1875-90 Chief Engineer of LCC 1890-1901.
Son of Alexander Binnie of London, born 26 March 1839 and died 18 May 1917.

Body, John B.

i/c Mexican Government Vera Cruz Harbour 1895-1902.
Resident Director Mexican Government Isthmus of Tehuantepec Harbours at Salina Cruz and Puerto Mexico (Coatzacoalcos) 1899-1909.
Director, S. Pearson & Son Ltd 1901.
Director, Mexican Eagle Oil Company 1909.
Possibly John Benjamin Body, born Mevagissey 1867, son of John Body, builder of Mevagissey and Leyton.
Carried the burden of the firm's large Mexican exploits from 1895 to 1919.

Brousson, Robert Percy

Director, Anglo-American Petroleum Products Company Ltd 1912.
Director, Eagle Oil & Shipping Company in 1931. Director Shell Mex & BP in 1935.
Electrical Engineer, son of Louis Maurice Brousson, author and editor, born 1871 in Sutton.

Carr, Herbert J.

Director, Anglo-American Petroleum Products Company Ltd 1912.

Cass, Bernard Croft
Director, S. Pearson & Son Ltd 1900.
i/c Main Drainage Outfall Dublin 1900.
Son of Sir John Cass, stuff manufacturer of Bradford, born 1873. Brother-in-law of Weetman Dickinson Pearson.

Chatterton, George
Consulting Engineer, Main Drainage Outfall Dublin 1900.
Sewage and Water Engineer, member of firm of Law and Chatterton, civil engineers.
Born c.1854 in Ireland and died 1910 in London.

Colls, A.
Secretary, Whitehall Securities Corporation Ltd 1907.
He joined S. Pearson & Son in 1891 and became company secretary in 1919.

Coode, Son & Matthews
Civil Engineers in Chief Admiralty Harbour Dover 1898.
Consulting Engineers London - a firm founded by Sir John Coode, Kt Bach 1872, KCMG 1886. President ICE 1889. Articled to James Meadows Rendel of Plymouth. Engineer in chief Portland Harbour Breakwater 1856-72, Member of Suez Canal Commission 1884-92. He was born in Bodmin, the son of Charles Coode, a solicitor, on 11 November 1816 and died in Brighton on 2 March 1892.

Diaz, Porfirio, General
President of Mexico 1876-1880, 1884-1911.
He first became president after a coup in 1876. In 1911 his increasingly dictatorial methods led to his overthrow whereupon he fled to Paris, having turned down Lord Cowdray's offer to use Paddockhurst, his house at Worth near Crawley. He died in Paris in 1915 aged 85. During his tenure of office he sold three quarters of the nation's mineral resources to foreign interests and apportioned millions of acres among friendly *hacendados* but nevertheless under his rule material prosperity grew and the country's public services infrastructure greatly improved.

Espinosa, Luis
Engineer, Valley of Mexico Main Drainage Channel 1889-1900.

Fox, (Charles) Douglas, Sir
Engineer, GN & City Railway 1898.
Engineer, Dorado Railway Extension Columbia 1905.
Civil Engineer and Contractor. President ICE 1899. Kt Bach 1886 for work in connection with Mersey Tunnel. Eldest surviving son of Sir Charles Fox, civil engineer, born 14 May 1840 and died 13 November 1921.

Fox, Francis
Engineer, GN & City Railway 1898.
Kt Bach 1912.Advisor to the Swiss Government for the construction of the Simplon Tunnel.
Brother of Sir Douglas Fox and son of Sir Charles Fox, civil engineer, born 1844 and died 7 Jan 1927.

Fraser, John
Engineer, Bradford Railway GNR 1864.
Civil engineer, articled to George Watson Buck, civil engineer. Chief Engineer of the Leeds, Bradford & Halifax Joint Railway by 1862. When this railway became part of the GNR in 1864 he was appointed District Engineer at Bradford. Born 28 July 1819 in Linlithgow, eldest son of James Fraser, architect of Manchester, and died at Leeds on 24 September 1881.

Gott, Charles
Engineer, Bradford Waterworks Oxenhope Tunnel 1870.
Engineer, Sheffield Main Drainage 1884.
Civil Engineer, Borough Surveyor, Bradford.
Son of Charles Gott, master bricklayer, born Great Grimsby, Lincolnshire, 1832 and died at Bradford 1908.

Harty, Spencer
Engineer, Main Drainage Outfall Dublin 1900.
Civil Engineer, Borough Surveyor and Waterworks Engineer Dublin, Hon Freeman 1907.
President ICE Ireland 1889.

Hopkinson, Frederick Thomas
i/c NER & Hull & Barnsley Ry Joint Dock Hull 1906.
Director, S. Pearson & Son Ltd 1912.
Civil Engineer, KBE 1925.
Son of James Hopkinson, contractor's clerk of Bury, Lancashire, born 1863 at Pewsey, Wiltshire, and died 19 September 1947.

Hunter, C.M.
General Manager, Santa Gertudis Jute Mill Company Ltd 1893.
Manager of the Jute Mills at Orizaba for 20 years.

Hyde, Clarendon Golding., Sir
Director, S. Pearson & Son Ltd 1897.
Director, Whitehall Securities Corporation Ltd 1907.
Chairman, Puebla Tramway Light and Power Company 1903.
Worked with the firm from 1888. Kt Bach 1910. Called to the Bar 1881. Liberal MP Wednesbury 1906-10.
Son of Henry B Hyde, Banker, born 5 February 1858 at Hampstead and died 24 June 1934.

Lavit, Emilio
Engineer, Mexican Government, Isthmus of Tehuantepec Harbours at Salina Cruz and Puerto Mexico (Coatzacoalcos) 1899-1909.
Engineer, Mexican Government Vera Cruz Harbour 1895-1902.

Limantour, Jose Yves
Finance Minister under President Diaz for 18 years.
He was the son of a Frenchman, Joseph Yves Lamantour and lived from 1854 to 1935. He reformed the fiscal system of Mexico and gave the country financial stability. He fell from power with Diaz in 1911.

Lyster, Anthony George
Engineer, Queens Branch Dock Liverpool 1902.
President, ICE. Engineer in chief Mersey Docks and Harbour Board from 1897 to 1913, succeeding his father, George Fosbery Lyster, who held the same post from 1861 to 1897. He was born in Holyhead in 1852 and died in 1920.

Macdonald, John H.
Director, Anglo-American Petroleum Products Company Ltd 1912.
Director, S. Pearson & Son Ltd 1919.
Chartered Accountant.

Mansergh, James

Engineer, Southport Main Drainage 1876.

Engineer, Plymouth Outfall Sewer 1904.

Civil Engineer specializing in sewage and freshwater schemes including the Elan Valley Reservoirs for Birmingham 1893. President ICE. Chairman 1901 of Engineering Standards Committee, which became the British Standards Institute.

Son of John Burkit Mansergh, linendraper of Lancaster, born 1834 and died 15 June 1905.

Masters, H.W.

Director, Anglo-American Petroleum Products Company Ltd 1912.

Meik, Patrick Walter

Engineer, Port Talbot Railway and Dock 1895.

Engineer, Seaham Harbour & Docks 1899.

Dock Engineer. In partnership with his father and brother, Charles Scott Meik, in Thomas Meik & Sons. Thomas Meik retired 1888 and the firm was renamed PW Meik and CS Meik in 1896.

Resident Engineer for foundations and piers of Forth Bridge 1883-6.

Son of Thomas Meik, a Scottish civil engineer, born 1851 at Bishopwearmouth and died 1910 at Westminster.

Moir, Ernest William

Director, S. Pearson & Son Ltd 1900.

i/c Pennsylvania Railroad New York Tunnel 1904.

Civil Engineer, created a baronet 11 July 1916. Resident Engineer for the southern cantilevers of the Forth Railway Bridge. Designer of tunnelling shield for Blackwall Tunnel 1892. Comptroller of Munitions Department, Ministry of Munitions 1915.

Son of Alexander M. Moir, general merchant of St Pancras, Middlesex, born 9 June 1862 and died 14 June 1933.

Mundy, E.H.

Director, Anglo-American Petroleum Products Company Ltd 1912.

Murray, Alexander William Charles Oliphant, Lord, of Elibank

Director, S. Pearson & Son Ltd 1912.

Liberal Member of Parliament for Midlothian from 1900-1905, Peebles and Selkirk from 1906-1910, and again for Midlothian from 1910-1912. He was Comptroller of Her Majesty's Household from 1905-1909 and Scottish Liberal Whip, 1906-1910; Under Secretary of State for India in 1909; Chief Liberal Whip, 1909-1912; Parliamentary Secretary to the Treasury, 1910 1912. Privy Counsellor 1911 and raised to the peerage as Baron Murray of Elibank in 1912.

Eldest son of Montolieu Fox Oliphant Murray, 1st Viscount and 10th Lord Elibank, born 12 April 1870 and died 13 September 1920.

Newell, Thomas M.

Engineer, NER & Hull & Barnsley Ry Joint Dock Hull 1906.

Civil Engineer, Dock Engineer NER Hull.

Son of Alderman John Newell JP, contractor of Bootle, born c.1863 Birkenhead.

Pawley, Richard

Engineer, NER & Hull & Barnsley Ry Joint Dock Hull 1906.

Civil Engineer, Chief Engineer Hull & Barnsley Railway.

Son of Richard James Pawley, Registrar to the Court of the Lord Mayor of London, born c.1857 Cheshunt, Hertfordshire.

Pearson, Clive Bernard

Director, Whitehall Securities Corporation Ltd 1907.

Chairman and Director, Anglo-American Petroleum Products Company Ltd 1912.

Director, S. Pearson & Son Ltd 1917.

Chairman, S. Pearson & Son Ltd 1927-54. Director Southern Railway 1936-47, Chairman British Overseas Airways Corporation 1940-43.

Second son of Weetman Dickinson Pearson, born 12 August 1887 and died 22 July 1965.

Pearson, Edward Ernest

Director, S. Pearson & Son Ltd 1900.

i/c Malta Dry Dock 1903 & Breakwater 1904.

i/c Valparaiso Harbour, Chilean Government, 1912. Responsible for construction HM Munitions factory, Gretna Green during First World War.

Kt Bach 1917, High Sheriff Hertfordshire 1909, Mayor of Hereford 1921-3.

Second son of George Pearson, born 10 May 1874 and died 19 November 1925.

Pearson, George

Partner, S. Pearson & Son 1856, retired 1895.

Son of Samuel Pearson, born 1833 Scholes and died 3 March 1899 at Brackendonbury, Hertfordshire.

Pearson, Samuel

Founder of firm 1844 which became S. Pearson & Son 1856. Retired 1879.

Farmer of Scholes near Cleckheaton, retired brickmaker in 1881 census.

Born 1814 died 1884.

Pearson, Weetman Dickinson, Sir, Viscount Cowdray

i/c Southport Main Drainage 1876.

Partner, S Pearson & Son 1879.

Director, S. Pearson & Son Ltd 1897.

Director & President, Whitehall Securities Corporation Ltd 1907.

MP for Colchester 1895-1910, President of Air Board 1917, High Steward of Colchester 1909, Rector Aberdeen University 1918-21. Created Baronet 1894, Baron Cowdray of Midhurst 1910, Viscount Cowdray of Cowdray 1917 PC 1917 GVCO 1925.

Elder son of George Pearson, born 15 July 1856 Shelley Woodhouse and died 1 May 1927 Echt, Aberdeenshire.

Pearson, Weetman Harold Miller, Major the Hon.

Director, Whitehall Securities Corporation Ltd 1907.

Director, S. Pearson & Son Ltd 1912.

MP for Eye 1906-18. 2nd Viscount Cowdray 1927.

Eldest son of Weetman Dickinson Pearson, born 18 April 1882 King's Lynn and died 5 October 1933 London.

Purdy, J.

Director, Anglo-American Petroleum Products Company Ltd 1912.

Rendel, Alexander Meadows, Sir

Engineer, Milford Haven Docks 1885.

Consulting Engineer to the India Office 1874, KCIE 1887. Works include Shadwell Basin, Albert Dock; Albert and Edinburgh Docks at Leith; Workington Dock and Harbour.

Son of James Meadows Rendel, FRS of Edinburgh, civil engineer, born 3 April 1829 at Plymouth and died 23 January 1918 in London.

Ritchie, Charles Thomson, Lord of Dundee

Chairman, Santa Gertudis Jute Mill Company Ltd 1893

MP for Tower Hamlets 1874-5, St Georges in the East 1885-92, Croydon 1895-1905, President Local Government Board 1886-92, Board of Trade 1895-1900, Home Secretary 1900-2, Chancellor of the Exchequer 1902-3. Rector of Aberdeen University 1902, created Baron 1905.

Son of William Ritchie of Broughty Ferry, born 19 November 1838 in Dundee and died 9 January 1906.

Ryan, W.B.

Vice President and General Manager, Tehuantepec National Railway opened 1906.

An American, son of John Ryan.

Stileman, Frank

Engineer, Cardiff Dry Docks 1895.

Civil Engineer.

Son of Francis Croughton Stileman, Chief Engineer Furness Railway, Harbours and Docks, born 1852.

Wake, Henry Hay

Engineer, Seaham Harbour & Docks 1899.

Served under Thomas Meik and, on his retirement in 1868, succeeded him as engineer to the River Wear Commission.

Son of William Morgan Wake, born 2 January 1844 Monkwearmouth and died 17 February 1911 Sunderland.

Walsh, Thomas Lister

i/c Valley of Mexico Main Drainage Channel 1889-1900.

i/c Seaham Harbour works 1899.

Civil Engineer. Son of John Walsh, solicitor's clerk of Halifax, born 1847.

Waters, Henry C.

Chairman, Tampico Electric Light Power & Traction Ltd 1912.

A British shareholder in *Compania de papel San Rafael y anexas* 1894, a lumber firm which used hydroelectricity.

Wilson, C.H.M.C.

Secretary, Anglo-American Petroleum Products Company Ltd 1912.

Secretary, Eagle Oil and Shipping Company 1931.

Worswick, A.E.

Engineer & General Manager, Mexican Hydro-Electric Companies.

A Canadian electrical engineer who built a 100 mile tramway system for Mexico City 1900.

Yorke, Vincent Wodehouse

Chairman, Vera Cruz Electric Light Power & Traction Ltd 1906.

Chairman of the Mexican Railway Ltd, Director Westminster Bank, Chairman National Provident Institution.

Son of John Reginald Yorke of Forthampton Court, Gloucester, born 21 May 1869 and died 27 November 1957.

Heraldry and other devices

Admiralty Office - seal
Gules an anchor in pale with a cable passing through the ring and environing the stock and fluke all or

America United States of
Or an eagle displayed in the dexter claw an olive branch and in the sinister a sheaf of three arrows the points upwards all proper from the beak a ribbon inscribed 'e pluribus unum' above the head encircled by clouds also proper as many molets of six points as there are States, on the body of the eagle a shield argent paly of six on a chief azure 13 molets of six points argent.

Bradford
Per pale gules and azure on a chevron engrailed between three bugle horns stringed or a well sable (granted 18 October 1847)

Bristol
Gules on the sinister side a castle of two towers domed all argent on each dome a banner charged with the cross of St George the castle on a mount vert the dexter base water all proper thereon a ship of three masts sailing from a port in the dexter tower her fore and main masts and rigging sable in full sail argent (recorded at a visitation in 1623)

Cardiff
Gules three chevronels or (unofficial arms. Cardiff did not get a grant of until 26 August 1906. These unofficial arms are perpetuated within the new arms)

Cass
Per pale argent and azure a balance suspended between two flaunches each charged with a branch of palm slipped all counterchanged (Arms granted to Bernard Croft Cass in the 1890s)

Colchester
Gules two staves raguly couped argent one in pale surmounted by another in fess between two ducal coronets in chief or the bottom part of the stave enfiled by a ducal coronet also or (granted by Letter Patent 7 July 1413)

Columbia
Azure on a fess argent between in chief a pomegranate or seeded gules between two cornucopias proper in base the Isthmus of Panama between two ships in full sail in the sea all proper a cap of liberty gules

Dublin
Azure three castles argent flammant proper (recorded at a visitation 1607)

Dublin Wexford & Wicklow Railway
Azure a harp or stringed argent
Supporters: Dexter - a lion rampant gardant crowned or
        Sinister - a unicorn argent horned tufted and crined reflexed over the back with a chain or
Motto: Erin go bragh
The shield is surmounted by a regal crown
(This is not the device that was normally used by the DW&WR on its rolling stock)

Egypt
Azure three molets of five points within the horns of a decrescent argent

England Arms
Gules three lions passant gardant in pale or

England Flag
Argent a cross gules (for St George)

Great Northern Railway
The arms of England conjoined with the arms of Scotland

Great Western Railway
The arms of London impaling the arms of Bristol

Guildford
Sable on a mount vert a castle with two towers embattled on each tower a spire from the battlements of the castle a tower triple towered all argent charged with an escutcheon of France quartering England under the battlements of the castle two roses in fess above a portcullis or the whole between two woolpacks in fess argent the base barry wavy argent and azure and over all in base a lion couchant gardant or

Ireland Arms
Azure a harp or stringed argent

Ireland Flag
Argent a saltire gules (earliest use 1567, a badge of the Order of St Patrick)

Kent
Gules a horse salient argent

Lancashire & Yorkshire Railway
The arms of Lancaster conjoined with the arms of York

Lancaster
Per fess azure and gules in chief a fleur de lis and in base a lion passant gardant or

Liverpool Docks, Seal of, 1811
A female figure seated on the bows of a ship and holding a laver branch while in front of her sits a Triton resting on a horn from which water gushes

London
Argent a cross gules in the first quarter a sword in pale point upwards argent
Supporters: Two dragons with wings elevated and addorsed argent charged on the wing with a cross gules
Crest: A dragon's sinister wing argent charged with a cross gules
(the arms and crest date back to 1359, the supporters to 1633)

London County Council, Seal of, 1889
A murally crowned female figure seated on a throne receiving gifts from two standing figures, dexter - a man, LABOUR and sinister - a woman, SCIENCE. Below an escutcheon bearing the arms of London (Arms not granted to the LCC until 29 July 1914)

Malta
Per pale argent and gules [a bordure or] (Admiralty Handbook of devices to be used on the Union flag by governors of colonies, territories, etcc.)

Mexico
Per pale vert and gules on a pale argent upon a rock in base proper a nopal plant or thereon an eagle in full aspect wings expanded holding in its beak a snake all proper
New York State device
In base a landscape over which the sun is rising in splendour

Middlesex
Gules three seaxes fessways argent pommels and hilts to the dexter or

New York City
Argent the sails of a windmill in saltire between two beavers passant in pale and two tuns in fess all proper
Supporters: Dexter - a sailor holding an oar in his dexter hand
          Sinister - a red Indian
Crest: Upon a demi-globe an eagle regardant wings expanded

NER and Hull & Barnsley Joint Dock
Azure three coronets in pale argent [for Hull] on a chief a 4-6-0 locomotive on the tender the letters NE H&B

Pearson
Per fess indented gules in chief two suns in splendour in base a demi griffin couped wings elevated and addorsed all counterchanged (granted to George Pearson in 1892)
Supporters: Dexter - a diver holding his helmet all proper
        Sinister - a Mexican peon proper
        (granted to Baron Cowdray in 1910)
Crest: In front of a demi griffin holding between its paws a millstone thereon a millrind sable a sun in splendour (granted to George Pearson in 1892)
Motto: Do it with thy might [Ecclesiastes viii10 - Whatsoever thy hand findeth to do, do it with thy might]

Plymouth
Argent a saltire vert between four towers sable (Arms recorded at a visitation in 1620)

Royal Arms
Quarterly of four 1 & 4 England 2 Scotland 3 Ireland

Scotland Arms
Or a lion rampant within a double tressure flory counter flory gules

Scotland Flag
Azure a saltire argent

Seaham
Four ermine spots conjoined in cross within a bordure indented or - Unknown

Sheffield
Per fess azure and vert in chief eight arrows in saltire banded argent in base three garbs or (Arms granted 1875)

Southport
Argent a fess dancetty between in chief three crosses crosslet in base a lifeboat under sail sky and sea all proper (unofficial arms)

Surrey Commercial Docks, Seal of, 1865
On a sea proper a three-masted boat in full sail argent masts and rigging or in base an anchor in pale argent with a cable or passing through the ring and environing the stock and fluke

Talbot
Crest: on a chapeau a lion statant or (Talbot)
Motto: Per Mare et Terram

Vera Cruz
Per fess vert and azure in base on a mound two pillars argent each enfiled by a ribbon the dexter bearing the word 'Plus' and the sinister 'Ultra' in chief resting on the pillars a castle domed or on the central dome a cross patonce proper inscribed with the word 'Vera' all within a bordure or hurty

Westminster
Azure a portcullis with chains pendant or on a chief or on a pale between two united roses of York and Lancaster the arms of King Edward the Confessor namely azure a cross patonce between five martlets one in each quarter and another in base all or

Whitehall Securities, Seal of, 1907
On a mount vert a representation of the Holbein Gate between two portcullises with chains pendant or in base a ribbon inscribed 1907

York
Argent on a cross gules five lions passant gardant or

Pedigree of Pearson

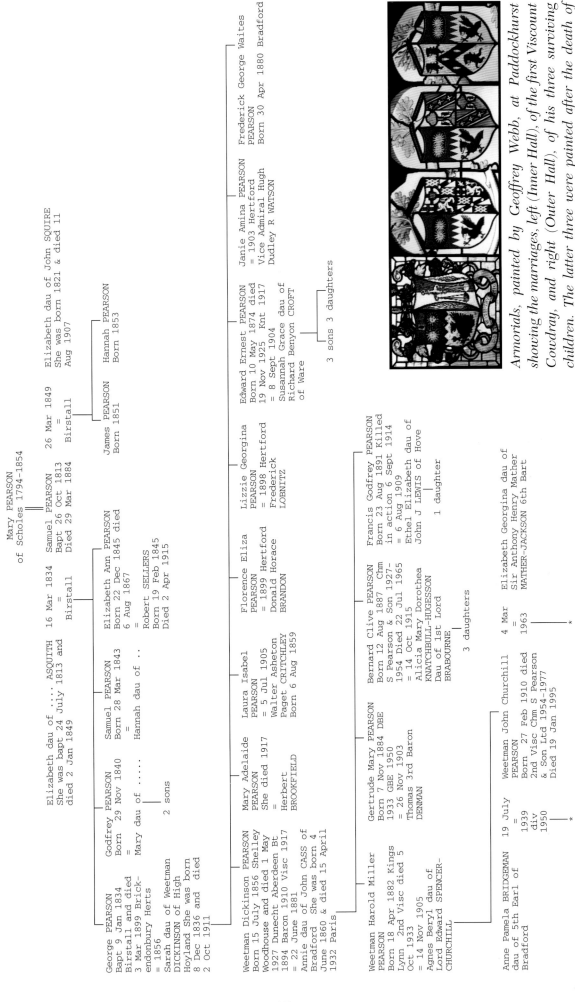

Mary PEARSON
of Scholes 1794-1854

Elizabeth dau of ..... ASQUITH She was bapt 24 July 1813 and died 2 Jan 1849 | 16 Mar 1834 Birstall | Samuel PEARSON Bapt 26 Oct 1813 Died 29 Mar 1884 | 26 Mar 1849 Birstall | Elizabeth dau of John SQUIRE She was born 1821 & died 11 Aug 1907

George PEARSON Bapt 9 Jan 1834 Birstall and died 3 Mar 1899 Brick-endonbury Herts = 1856 Sarah dau of Weetman DICKINSON of High Hoyland She was born 8 Dec 1836 and died 2 Oct 1911

Godfrey PEARSON Born 29 Nov 1840 = Mary dau of ...... 2 sons

Samuel PEARSON Born 28 Mar 1843 = Hannah dau of ..

Elizabeth Ann PEARSON Born 22 Dec 1845 died 6 Aug 1867 = Robert SELLERS Born 19 Feb 1845 Died 2 Apr 1915

James PEARSON Born 1851

Hannah PEARSON Born 1853

Edward Ernest PEARSON Born 10 May 1874 died 19 Nov 1925 Knt 1917 = 8 Sept 1904 Susannah Grace dau of Richard Benyon CROFT of Ware — 3 sons 3 daughters

Janie Amina PEARSON = 1903 Hertford Vice Admiral Hugh Dudley R WATSON

Frederick George Waites PEARSON Born 30 Apr 1880 Bradford

Weetman Dickinson PEARSON Born 15 July 1856 Shelley Woodhouse and died 1 May 1927 Dunecht Aberdeen Bt 1894 Baron 1910 Visc 1917 = 22 June 1881 Annie dau of John CASS of Bradford She was born 4 June 1860 & died 15 April 1932 Paris

Mary Adelaide PEARSON She died 1917 = Herbert BROOKFIELD

Laura Isabel PEARSON = 5 Jul 1905 Walter Asheton Paget CRITCHLEY Born 6 Aug 1859

Florence Eliza PEARSON = 1899 Hertford Donald Horace BRANDON

Lizzie Georgina PEARSON = 1898 Hertford Frederick LOBNITZ

Weetman Harold Miller PEARSON Born 18 Apr 1882 Kings Lynn 2nd Visc died 5 Oct 1933 = 14 Nov 1905 Agnes Beryl dau of Lord Edward SPENCER-CHURCHILL

Gertrude Mary PEARSON Born 7 Nov 1884 DBE 1933 GBE 1950 = 26 Nov 1903 Thomas 3rd Baron DENMAN

Bernard Clive PEARSON Born 12 Aug 1887 Chm S Pearson & Son 1927-1954 Died 22 Jul 1965 = 14 Oct 1915 Alicia Mary Dorothea KNATCHBULL-HUGESSON Dau of 1st Lord BRABOURNE — 3 daughters

Francis Godfrey PEARSON Born 23 Aug 1891 Killed in action 6 Sept 1914 = 6 Aug 1909 Ethel Elizabeth dau of John J LEWIS of Hove — 1 daughter

Anne Pamela BRIDGEMAN dau of 5th Earl of Bradford | 19 July = 1939 div 1950 * | Weetman John Churchill PEARSON Born 27 Feb 1910 died 2nd Visc Chm S Pearson & Son Ltd 1954-1977 Died 19 Jan 1995 | 4 Mar = 1963 | Elizabeth Georgina dau of Sir Anthony Henry Mather MATHER-JACKSON 6th Bart *

* 1 son and 2 daughters from each marriage

Armorials, painted by Geoffrey Webb, at Paddockhurst showing the marriages, left (Inner Hall), of the first Viscount Cowdray, and right (Outer Hall), of his three surviving children. The latter three were painted after the death of Francis Godfrey Pearson in September 1914.

Acknowledgements

This booklet would not have been written if Barbara Mulroy, knowing my interest in Railway Heraldry, had not arranged in 1995 for me to visit the Pearson Room in the Brunswick Building of Leeds Metropolitan University. On seeing such a spectacular display I was overwhelmed and was, subsequently, invited to give a talk to the Yorkshire Heraldry Society on the story behind the windows. After repeating the talk to three other heraldry societies there the matter lapsed until 2005. In December that year the stained glass panels moved with the School of the Built Environment to their new home in Queen Square Court. In the Pearson Corridor, more prominently displayed than before, much interest in the panels was engendered and many questions were asked about them which could not be readily answered.

Veronica Lovell, a colleague of Barbara Mulroy, remembering my earlier involvement, contacted me for information. This resulted in an invitation from Jane Kettle, Head of the School of the Built Environment, to look at the panels in their new position. At this visit I offered to write a small booklet that would record, as far as possible, a complete history of the stained glass and how it got to Leeds. Much to my surprise, Jane readily acceded to this suggestion.

Now, with the prospect of my knowledge of the windows achieving the permanence of the printed word, I revisited my previous researches into S. Pearson & Son Ltd. and found new avenues to explore. These revealed a fuller and more accurate picture. To achieve this result I have been helped by a number of people: Veronica Lovell, who located the Leeds Polytechnic papers covering the circumstances of the windows arrival in Leeds; Jenny Lynch, assistant archivist at the House of Lords Library, and Dr Mark Collins, Estates Archivist of the Parliamentary Estates Directorate, who provided me with information about the Whitehall Club and its subsequent history; Christopher Talbot-Ponsonby of English Heritage who located photographs of the windows in their original home: Peter O'Donoghue, Bluemantle Pursuivant, who provided details of the Grant of Arms to George Pearson: Father Bede Hill and Father Patrick Fludder of Worth Abbey (Paddockhurst) who photographed the Cowdray armorials there. I am also grateful to Kath Hatfield for reading the manuscript and finding my slips of grammar, punctuation and syntax and to Becky Riley, PA to Jane Kettle, for the help I have received from her. Finally this booklet would not have materialised in such a splendid form without the computer publishing skills of Ian Dickinson.

I also owe a huge (posthumous) debt of gratitude to John Alfred Spender (1862-1942), editor of the *Westminster Gazette* from 1896 to 1922 and biographer of Lord Cowdray. His book *Weetman Pearson, First Viscount Cowdray, 1856-1927*, published in 1930. is a mine of useful information, about both the viscount and the firm that he led to such prominence in public works contracting.